Maskwork

Maskwork

Gregory Leadbetter

Nine
Arches
Press

Maskwork
Gregory Leadbetter

ISBN: 978-1-913437-03-9
eISBN: 978-1-913437-04-6

First published September 2020 by:

Nine Arches Press
Unit 14, Sir Frank Whittle Business Centre,
Great Central Way, Rugby.
CV21 3XH
United Kingdom

www.ninearchespress.com

Nine Arches Press is supported using public funding by Arts Council England.

Supported using public funding by
ARTS COUNCIL
ENGLAND

For my teachers

'muses, goddesses of learning'
– *A Table Alphabeticall* (1604)

Contents

Well — but what *is* this *now* and yet *other* World?
— **Samuel Taylor Coleridge**

Man is least himself when he talks in his own person.
Give him a mask and he will tell you the truth.
— **Oscar Wilde**

the true mask is the expression of somebody unmasked
— **Peter Brook**

Maskwork

To teach the mask I make
  to tell the truth, I wear it
  as my own: feel its weight tilt
when it sees the first earthly thing
it loves suffer in its infant being:
  one mask passes to another
  the face that it has learned.
Still it makes no sound, even as
  its senses sow their trance
  where what would be its language grows.
Only when my life has done its work
  and the mask knows more than I could say
  without its visage – then
I take it off. It wears my voice:
  the mask speaks.

Musician

That night plays back scratched vinyl,
but here's my fiddle.

The lane led way out and I went
though dark had spilt and shook the stars
in black water where I walked,
dressed for day and led by story,
nothing more. The spirits I'd swilled
warmed my blood, but the cold drank.
I knew I didn't have long before
the blue moon stilled my flesh to crystal.

I heard it come: the air at work,
the medium lipping my ears and mouth,
spittled fingers circling my skin
to make it ring. I felt the bow
I'd hung at my back grow taut
and the raw strings of what you call
my *violin* thrill for the kiss:
they braced to meet and make a voice.

And then I was there: the blind road
emptied into a field, as if
where I stepped a sudden breath
had blown the earth to a sphere of glass.
I met that world's musician:
a white moth alight within
its whisper. One of us said
play, and I did, and what it spoke
I learned, even as it danced me
to the bone in sound that shivered
to a mute dawn. I woke under dew
in open ground. I had no home.

You don't have to believe me, but I can tell
your body heard. The song gets through.
That's how I got this tune on my tongue.

Doe

Inside the green rhythm
below rippling leaves, turned
from the squint of a sickly heat,
the doe and I were breath

held in exchange for a sense
not yet our own but
heard in a call from the nerve
of this wood, spoken as a bird

that lit the feathered shade
we stepped into as space
we fell and flew towards
each time we stopped to tilt an ear

to listen for the trail of the other's voice.
I tried to speak the name for *friend*
and the sound came back as the bark
of trees point-blank at my skin

that let me slip like a finger
through their silent folds
teaching my touch
to hatch like an egg.

Don't be afraid I almost said
if not to myself, to the verging dead,
bone-dust scattered in bluebells,
deathbells knelling death's end

in the sough of the wild
that led her and me,
sly as lovers, into this secret
taut as a web.

We opened like flowers, our scent
thickening air moist
with the dew of our lungs,
limned with antennae

fed on the dark light
of the radiant body afoot or sweet
with rot where it fell. We flickered
like a tongue from an adder's jaw

and flared at our meeting, revealed.
The doe startled from her mottle bed
as if, this time, I had spoken
her true name, and fled.

A Poppet

When I dug you up
like a potato,
you could have been
vegetable, grown
in earth too long

lost by a girl
who gave you her name
and worried her parents
to death with her love
for your unstitched eyes

whose loose threads
look into mine
as I bath you until
the water is black
and your human hair

is chestnut again,
and the hemp sac
of your skin is warm
from the fire I
nearly put you in.

The embers are cold
when I think I wake
to find you folded
into my bed
and your voice thrown

to the tilth of my garden
growing you bone
by bone with words
no human breath
could hold, biting

my tongue and drawing
blood that tastes
wrong as I follow,
now a father
to a lost child

and feel small hands
push me into
fresh-torn ground.
When I think I wake,
your small hands lift me out.

Gramarye

I want speech that makes my skin
more than the book I have made
of its membrane
    silent as lips
    at the mouth
that leans from the air

   and this is how
that work in my flesh began:
the desire that drew me like sap
to its tip, where I hung by my voice
    from the whispering ash
    that grew in the garden
    it made of my death
for runes cut by the tongue to touch
every beginning that is to come
to the egg from which I was born.

I learned to know love by the names that I made
and the names took bodies of their own
that glistered with the dust of their home:
unblinking at the strangeness of what I had done
in piercing their silence, sending my voice
to open as an iris under their sun:
they pluck it from the pulsing earth and come.

I have woken to moonlight leaking from the wound:
    the skin that I speak with
    fresh with the blood of its wish.

Two Lost Things

E.A.L. at four years old

She dreamt of two lost things,
their cobweb feathers soft to touch,
perched, as if for food, or such
thin fare as dreaming brings
to wean two wisps with wings,
the orphans of their clutch.
Their song is nothing, and too much:
silence twinned with that which sings.

She does not name these darlings
of the dark that came to land
on her, light as fledglings,
the spinning air's awakenings.
She comes to me to understand.
'Look,' she says, holding out her hand.

Cara

She has no tongue: it withered without her
        being born.
I might have sung to her –
        heard her
sing back a scuffed phonograph
        of baby-speech
foreign as a language
        never formed
but mouthing at the gauze
        of being.
Not even a memory of skin
        brushes mine,
her absence is so soft
        to touch.
She hides too well: not even a shadow
        could find her,
and only her mother and father
        would look.
It must be her hunger that I feel
        in her place,
though I am full and she has nowhere
        to feed.
The sway of words will not move her silence
        or make her walk.
There is no earth to lay her: she is not as real
        as the dead.
She is barely a thing that might have been
        my daughter, or son.

Labels for the Exhibition of an Hitherto Private Cabinet of Masks

A mask for the opening of the mouth
        where death has occluded the breath.

A mask in the figure of an emerald moth
        emergent from the pupa of the head.

A mask torn from a seraph
        as it fled to its vacuum.

A mask of sticks in the likeness of a man
        found in use as the nest of a bird (species uncertain).

A mask lifted from the bark of a pear at Wyre
        said to weep sap from the cut of its eyes.

A mask taken from a witch in the likeness of a wren
        (said to have revealed her human form).

A mask like to the head of a devilfish
        fetched from the sea at Candia.

A mask in the likeness of a sleeping child
        donated by its mother.

A mask of alabaster in the likeness of the collector
        as he was last seen in this life.

Metaphysician

After she died, my grandmother told me
that I was a healer. You could say that
I retired at forty. It's hard to stay true
to the truth of a dream, but I have
my work. Let me clear you a space
by the fire. I like a room with a touch
of Prometheus: it reminds me
of my purpose here, alone with only
his gift and the broken clay
of human faces. The antique globe
in the corner is as close as I get
to the world that I left, the dysfunction
I failed to solve, for all I had learned
from my own wound. An astrologer
once told me that Venus was conjunct
with Chiron in the House of my calling:
a trinity of love, hurt and healing
in my hands. All I will say is, I recognised
the person she described. Here we are
in my cave of mysteries. I repair
beautiful things that are still or silent
with age or neglect: things that – like language –
others have made in time out of mind,
that now might stoop broke-necked or try to see
with one glass eye. It's a delicate task,
but the results can astonish even me.
Last week I woke an ibis made of silver
and mother-of-pearl, and heard it speak
of the Da'at of Cabala before
I watched it go, anxious as a parent
for a child. All my favourites house a daemon.
One, baroque as a fairground fortune-teller,

I call 'The Poet'. He can only speak
one poem – and then only if I lend him
my breath. It's a good poem, you'd enjoy it.
Others play music like you've never heard,
as if Orpheus really could make stone
stir. So you see, I haven't given up
on what my grandmother told me after
she died, though I've grown as strange as my art.
You are the first to wonder who I am,
so for you I will do something different.
Give me the music box you have brought.
Thank you. I can see that it's close to your heart.
Sometimes the fix is in the flaw.   There.
Open it: listen. The dancer, lithe
as a living flame, is the prime mover:
everything around her rises to dance.

Tree Script

Turn the key to the mouth
in your hand, the wand in the leaves
of your voice, grown to your ear
from the ground, to your eye from the bough
that roots in the tilth of the sky:
let these be signs that grow
with mind where mind is sown:

In flower the first   *Apple*
has the scent of all letters:
the fruit and drunkenness
of speech in the juice of its flesh
at the lips: the first letter
is a kiss.

Its blossom makes an Easter-month   *Cherry*
that dances from itself.

For birth, a conifer: *Fir*
an egg of many seed-heads
balanced impossibly
on its branch.

Each branch a tree   *Cedar of Lebanon*
to house a heaven
and its shadow.

A shadow spells with the ink of a moon   *Birch*
until its fingers thin to twigs:
tap the pale skin and drink:
its blood is sweet.

A thicket hides a path and a girl   *Blackthorn*
who said 'I'll go the blackthorn way.'

She lights a fire at the leaf   *Rowan*
that song-birds swallow
and burn as song.

What once was a hedge   *Hawthorn*
huddled between worlds
is a fragrant sex.

The black buds of morning   *Ash*
unclasp: lovers hang on beauty
open-mouthed.

Eyes wake in their shimmering skin: *Beech*
a rack of antlers lifts from the mast
as if the book of skin could speak:
a temple rises from a knot of snakes.

Its leaves are an acre of light   *Lime*
for bees in the cloud of their wings:
its bark is the mask of a moth.

Read the double that grows from the lip   *Alder*
in the mirror of water: the topmost branch
of this world whistles
to the other.

Its sprays are silver-green whispers   *Willow*
twisted from the air
to blow a word
beyond its breath:
'The Moon owns it.'

Walk through the midsummer door   *Oak*
to wear the common crown
that outlives any monarch:
an oracle nests in your hair.

Pour this tree along your body   *Olive*
to glister like sap in the oil of the sun:
the fissures of age grow young.

Under the lobes of its leaves   *Fig*
the pendant head
purples with sugars.

A sage old as incarnation   *Plane*
sloughs the fools of time in flakes.

A hand gloved in honeydew   *Sycamore*
falls from the ooze of the shade
as if to follow the wing of a seed.

A shape swells in a green flame: *Hazel*
the truth can be eaten
straight from the stave.

A balm for the living   *Elder*
to revive the dead:
they are crushed together
in a black wine.

A white flower   *Ivy*
bursts from a wreath
marrying leaf to leaf.

Touch the tip of the green spine: *Holly*
the year with its head
cut off is alive.

The vanished letter   *Elm*
is voiced in tacit.

The trembling torch   *Poplar*
of the light of day
is passed underground
by a buried hand.

A figure blooms   *Yew*
in the bleeding dark:
brings your finger to her lips:
begins to write.

Archaeopteryx

Not the folded bone and feather, but the word
had taken hold: a fossil angel
echo splitting open that first syllable,
the optics exposed in the sound I heard:

before I knew, something spoken now stirred
a tongue in stone, elastic and audible,
my English cleaving to its alien kernel
at work in the absence of the first bird.

I remember this, and the story you told:
a visit to the Natural History Museum,
the reptile wing as living as dead,

my language as young as its grain was old:
you, wondering at your infant son,
the attendant, startled at what I said.

Two Friends

i.m. Andy Payne (1961-2016)

Two friends might have this kind
of conversation: it takes the form
of an unfinished thought, warm
with what the two might find

just by carrying on their talk,
over the hedge or over a beer,
like idlers on an evening walk:
two friends content to live so near.

There is always something more to say,
always something left unfinished
when these two go their way,
and this the two friends cherished –

and so their conversation carries on
even when one of the two has gone.

Personal Computing

I slot the rewound cassette into the deck:
   type LOAD, press PLAY▶.
The monitor flickers its glitch
   rainbow, begins to unscramble
its data with a sound like a signal
   scratched from the depth of space.
I am maybe nine years old,
   and you, Dad, can't be far away.
This is a Commodore 64,
   its console the colour of praline fondant,
the second computer in the quiet
   revolution you brought to our home
that for us had begun with the VIC-20:
   20KB of read-only memory,
new words with their strange promise –
   the hope hard-wired in the dream
of tech – and that, I think, is what
   you loved in these: the greater human
good that we might make with them,
   the computer as a kind of friend
to help our thinking grow.
   The next one you bought was the Amiga 500
with 1MB and a built-in disc-drive
   and *that* felt like the future.
The revolution got faster: after the Commodores
   you built your own, but eventually
the Windows PC won out, leaving
   the house a clutter of computer
archaeology. Look at us now.
   You and I might have discussed
the quantum mechanics of dementia:
   how you can be here and not here

at once. If I had kept those old
   computers, might they one day
remake you from skin cells
   smudged from your thumb
on the mould of your mouse –
   left-click your mind to life
again? But it wouldn't be you.
   The future has come and gone.
I am still watching the flickering screen
   waiting for all we have lost to load.

Lapse

You're in the daze of a garden
where you've sat too still
for too long. A bee is drunk
in the cup of a flower, abuzz
with its anther. The grasses
are taller than when you last
looked. Their heads lean over
heavy with seed like a primitive
wheat you might gather to begin
again from where you are,
loosened from time by the drug
of summer, not a man, not a
child, but watching the mouths
of the foxglove slowly open
to both, like those who watch
from the far side of the speed of light
who see our sun as a star.

Apple Tree

My apple tree reads like a palm
    of time out of mind
    to touch
in the flickering shadow of its sun
    fingering
    in the crust of bark
    wounds so open and hospitable
            to moss and friend
          each web and stretch of mucus silvering
          emmet-ways through cracked striations
    eyes of mouths too old to speak
        except in seedling
           snakeskin green
      as old as that first garden where
I travel inside
    the sphere of its full bloom
        fragrant with first knowledge

If I could kiss the tree I would
but instead touch my lips
    to the cloud of wings
         its boom of pollen
    woos from the air
hang blessings from the flowering spurs
    that maze the sky
    where birds fly in to stow
       like secrets growing leaf and song
    never pruned of its confusion
       this year like the last it is
       too deep into another season
unhelped by human hands
    that lift children to its ragged seat
    and canopy of rustling stars
       writing out the swelling fruit

Optics

I would not leave the light alone
until it gave and swallowed me
and made the sun as soft as air
that turned my body like a key

I would not leave the light alone
until I winkled out a bee
to catch the petal of my eye
and lift its pollen pupil free

I would not leave the light alone
until the heaven of earth looked back
and held my face as if it heard
the voice that drinks the bright star black

I would not leave the light alone
until it cooled into eclipse
and washed the mortal skin from me
like water poured to parted lips

I would not leave the light alone
until I felt it crack and tilt
its crazing hive of compound eyes
to mirror my diffracted guilt

I would not leave the light alone
until the sudden shadow crisped
each dumbstruck leaf and shuttered green
to brimstone where the serpent kissed

I would not leave the light alone
until the lucence of its yolk
had fed the limpid human mould
and wound a self within its smoke

I would not leave the light alone
until a sound could pass as clear
through me as sky that scatters blue
to shatter us with what we hear

I would not leave the light alone
until I wore it like a mark
and now the teeming eyes it wakes
come surging through the open dark

The Swoops

I hold on as the sun takes me down,
down all the way to the home of the lost
who come now, the swoops that circle and sound
the depth of their hunger, find me cast
in the tacit mould of their song.

Found in a Wood

No more than fifty paces from the path
    that overlaid the disused track
I broke through scrub to scabby willow
    until I had no trail to follow.

I found a bed in a fallen trunk:
    a sleeping bag in its damp crust.
A fire of sticks, bottles and pages torn
    from a book had lit and burned.

I read what was left of one blackened leaf:
    words the flames had refused to speak.
The way was lost and I was alone.
    'Don't you want to go home?'

Engine Pool, Earlswood Lakes

Neither town nor country
but their breach in each other

and the sump of winter
spilling its rupture:

the familiar lake drained to its floor,
gashed to gulls and shallows

and what was drowned exposed.
The new wild speaks no reason.

I walk into the vanished water
and the white noise

of the motorway travelling
under the horizon.

A moorhen calls
from the cleft in the air

and the broken symmetry
of swan mussel shells

lifts from the deeper silt,
each a splintered wing.

Fires have been lit on the false shore
for the missing world:

their ashes join the industrial grit
that sifts the waste as food.

A glass bottle from the last century –
Maclean Brand Stomach Powders –

marks what looks too like a grave:
a low cairn of brick and stone

the length of a man, blackened
as if from a crude pyre,

now a cold hearth.
The lake brims

with its revenant.
Footprints come and go.

Tuisto

In their ancient songs, which are their only records or annals, they celebrate the god Tuisto, sprung from the earth... – Tacitus, *Germania*

take *eorþe*, a single cell
that tongues upon
itself, a worm
until it scrapes its likeness
out of shape
and the howl that calls the split world back
is found

cannot be stopped,
had already begun

to pair wings,
the envy of the lungs,
make them swooping mandibles

the bite
of finger and thumb

ghost of the bean
that flings two tendrils, root and stem
to lash suckling soil
to greening sky

the grasp of the spore
on broken skin

the love that breeds
in meat left out

the glut of symmetry
spilling through birth

that hammers snake-legs into bronze,
loops and folds fishtail feet
to mantis arms, raised
to grip the fork of horns

heads that grow
with the geometry of leaves

the double helix of his gaze
spiralling each beast apart

he is laughing
in the beating heart, both one
and two and two within

he draws a nerve without a name
but with your face
from the seething mere,
coupled eyes that drip back
to the black mud
that looks up into the same glaze,
drops its jaw,
wants to speak but can only lick
through open lips

O creator of the kiss

Modranect

The year reverses into life:
the sky a death of indigo
before the utter bloom of dark
is born without words again

Just bare tact for the indrawn breath
of light steeping blind roots
for the spring of his blood to blossom
in a hidden season green with tongues

Leaves dance to the earth
damp at his lips to bud
in black soil rifted with limbs
that rise from the pit of the sun

Eyebright leaks from the sleep
and dust of reason
where the quiet of healing
grows close to disease

The wren travels the length of night
hungry for the stars
she pecks as crumbs
from the paths to heaven

No prayers are left unspoken
in reverse at the speed of creation
clattering back into the laughter
in which he first heard the ghost of god

Solstice, Midwinter

Now the sun is the shining stone of a moon
cool on the skin and film of the eye.

It breathes the earth to mist as light
and gives the skull its star to hold.

Sleepery

To sleep, they lead you
　　　　　by the hand
　　　　　　　of your shadow
　　　from screen-
　　　　　　blenched light
like a pregnant body
　　　　　to a hatchery
　fit for the last of your species.

They do not speak
　　　　　　but the soft wash
　　　　　　　　of the billowing walls
　　　is steeped and warm
　　　　　with breath before
　　　　　　a thought

and you know
　　　　　　you are already in the birthing phase
　of the farthest form
　　　　　of enhanced sleep
　　　　　　　after so long a gestation
　　　　alone
　　　at the brink of the flesh
　　　　　you share
　　　　　　　with everyone

and brace for the paradox
　　　　　you came for
　　　　　to come:
　　　　　　　the union with wakefulness
　　　　　　　that will make the new human.

Your eyes open.
　　　　　They do not blink.

Transhumanist Glitch

You've done what toddlers are told not to do
and blown yourself halfway across the room.
You've probably fried your favourite nanode.
Give us both a minute. Don't try to speak.
That's it, sit up. Here's your food. Now suck.

I was thinking about how all this began.
The trail leads back to a bad metaphor.
I don't mean the word we stole from the poets –
'transhuman', Cary's inspired rendering
of Dante's godlike leaven – though it's theirs.

No, I mean the way we identified
our very being with a tool we invented:
'software' for the dark energy of thought,
'hardware' for flesh still growing from its root.
The computer cast a primitive glamour

back in the day: the stuff you can do with IF
THEN commands! It makes me laugh, to think
how we thought we could code the magic herb
that Glaucus found – make ourselves immortal…
that old lure. H+! What clichés we were.

It wasn't so high-minded, either: sex
tends to find a way, as your ridiculous
pizzle can testify. But what stings now
is that we couldn't cope with not knowing
what we are. We couldn't live unprogrammed.

Bad metaphors breed bad science. And love?
Ha. You're all I've got. And we haven't been right
since the upload went wrong, left me half in,
half out. Like this. On your feet. You're a putz.
That mask in the mirror won't do for a smile.

The Ape at the End of the World

I set the alarm, though I won't wake again.
Habits die harder than humans, I find.
I wonder if Oupsi will switch it off –
she's seen me do it a thousand times –
or simply regard it, the ways she looks
at what she's learned to live with, but doesn't
understand: her heavy brows lifting as her
eyelids slightly narrow, almost sleepy
in her mild query, the way she might look
at me after I haven't moved for a day
or two, assuming she stays that long.
The Earbud told me a story once
about a dog that stayed by the corpse
of its owner for weeks. I don't think
an orang would do that. They know that life
goes on. That it already has.
                                    I'm glad
to have Oupsi, hunkered on her branch,
not too far from the fire I set for the night,
nor from me in the last of my blankets.
She's munching the last of the figs.
The Earbud, they promised, would never lose charge.
My teacher, my friend: the Earbud made me
the stunted philosopher I am.
It taught me how to look after Oupsi –
how to find her out here, my extinction-
sister – and I'm grateful for that.
                                    The tech
says forever, but the flesh knows better.
And the tech turns out to be flesh, after all:
a black pebble I tap from my head
like the scorpion I tipped from my boot.
Summa sapientiae! I know you
at last.

I call Oupsi down by her name,
which I gave her to remind me of our
little disaster. *Oupsi*, I say,
and she comes – as if the undoing
of the undoing we've done – as if
I saw the mistake before it happened
and by making that sound, like a prophet
I could make the correction in time.
Oupsi, I say.
                    She comes. She has finished
her fig, so she's curious. We hug.
I want to give her something to remember
me by. I blow the red dust from the Earbud.
Oupsi, I say, this is for you. The fire
flickers her eyes. She picks up the Earbud
between finger and thumb, puts it to her mouth –
as if to think with her lips – and spits it
like a pip. She turns and climbs back to her bough.
I put my head to the earth. I know
she won't hear that alarm.

At Porlock Salt Marsh

Powders of bone
rise like ash
ghost the grasses
in the dust of a moon

the bled-cold sun
foams into embers
rolls under cloud
on flint-struck sea

reeds electric
with an insect fuse
voice the air
with the discharged land

to know what it is
to be where I am
I touch the white stone
to the tip of my tongue

Interval

Another attempt at silence fails.
We name the rift between our speech
and not the want of sound. In this,
silence wakes the genes of unheard
things that crowd where words have been.
You don't have to take a vow to change
your life. But who are you? Without
a voice to muzzle the roaring world
you hear your heart fend for itself,
the tinnitus of your singing nerve.
I found a place where cars and planes
were silent too, the air stilled
to standing water clear enough
to drink, and all my body drank.
A gnat at the distant lip of the land
flared aloud, fed on the pulse
of earth. For a while I couldn't return.
The closer you come to silence, the further
it recedes. I am far from you right now,
at work on something lonely.
I hope the language is listening.

Sakadas at Delphi

A plaine and easie introduction to practicall musicke

What was it that spoke, to draw a dancer
        like a thread from the air –
        enough to make the aether we breathe its own –
to blow a tongue of light through black stone
        faster than reason –
that drew me to the spiral of the dance it sang,
        a spirit raised
in the fume and folds of its pyre
        of silence?

To tamper with being –
        a touch at the hollows of our bones
        that moves a roomful of statues to life
            in hearing?

I set my feet to its secret
        and follow.
Wary, too, of what I might wake
        as I cut the reed from the mirror of the lake
        and listen for the shadow of a jealous god
            to run its blade
            along my skin.
        They want the same thing:
            to sound beyond speech.

What I heard was older than fear or pleasure –
        true before the breaking of the world
        into question and answer.
We are its theatre.

These pipes, these reeds at my lips
        make a voice
        like fire, a blur
of creature and creator.

I tutor your children
        in the body of the dancer.
Have you come
        like the stars at your shoulder
                to listen?

        Good.

Now you are still, and the air, like an ear to an oracle, open.

Terroir

A tasting I didn't expect –
Livery Street in the bowl of a Burgundy glass:
on the nose, something sour
as I step at first through a subway:
something gouty, a boiled kidney
and something spilt, on a cold tile,
a chemistry teacher would call
the colour of straw:
piquant as iron –
that's *livery*, I suppose,
gravied with onion:
then I get the grumble of a train, delayed:
exhaust, but not diesel, unleaded:
and now, a smokehouse:
the vapour of garam masala,
the grey slate of concrete
someone compared to the stone slopes of Mosel –
and, at the back of my tongue,
behind the dried fish of Lithuania,
the fade of that lonely song by Charlotte Gainsbourg
that I heard just once.

All this – *Indicazione Geografica Tipica* –
and then you're in
with a hint of arabica
under the warm barrel of arch thirteen
and enter something Bacchic:
just a breath of Baron Bigod cheese:
the promise of appassimento bliss.
La Chablisienne rests a smile on your shoulder:
Madame Bollinger asks
Where have you been?

Someone sips, an apothecary
at their own potion –
and then, well met,
the world at my lips,
so do I: today
an Alicante Bouschet.

Beorma

Begin with the dark Beorma knew
and bring a hammer-blow of light:
our tongues are metals

struck in the centuries of our mouths,
priceless alloys of a plural English,
word-hoard of the world:

through Bromwycham and Brummagem,
the grove and ley of Brom,
the ore of all that has been sung

by fire from that first night
domed by the stars of new-found land
to the city now, no single sound

can speak – whose chord claims us
as its own, asks us what we want
to keep and what rebuild

forever the city never still
but sprung at its own making:
city of a thousand glossal

greens that breathe for every machine,
the way that words, whether known
or wanted, speak for speechless things –

born to the brink of the voice
we have but never wholly learn:
our daily task of new invention.

Begin with the wonders of your home
and they will come: light the gas-blue flame
of a kingfisher's flight along the Cole.

Unconscious Minister

*The reader may choose to think of him as, possibly, no more
than a sublunary druggist; it may be so, but my faith is better.
I believe him to have evanesced...* – Thomas De Quincey

The flicker of tallow for a mind
    brought back
    half-willing
to be damned
    having seen
    such light
through three wounds to the head
    of seed
    that leak
their offering, blend with wine
    suffer mouths
    obscene with mulberry
tongues to speak abandon
    into the void
    of speech
to drink and from those lips
    be drunk
    and doubled flesh

The manikin of a stammering day
    that tries to be
    two worlds at once
that each forbid the other
    drowning Sunday
    city street
a body but this vanished one
    as lost as fast
    as it is found
this voice between its staring eyes

Dérive

Turn around three times and walk. Start
   now. The atlas skimmed by a gust on the charity stall
was out of date before it got soaked
   and its borders and crossings were spilt
by a lick of November rain. It was only one story
   half-told, as any map will tell you.
The sign read backwards is *Doowylloh*
   which spools a film in misheard Welsh
from the faint cry of my missing ancestry.
   But look at this England, under the weather:
a carrot grows through a lost ring,
   turdus philomelos sings out of season.
A hoarding for hot pork rolls ripped off by the show
   of a storm wraps my legs: a tired *Oh Christ*
sorry, and I say *OK* and carry on for my train
   which I hope is late so I can get 'home'.
The only hedgehog I've seen for ten years
   is a skid on the road a few car-lengths
from the front door, and a carved pumpkin-head
   from the month before has burst with a kick
and been walked into patched-up tarmac where
   I take my daughter to school and we listen to starlings
twirl from their bough and the moon, like the earth
   seen from the lunar surface, gives back what we see
and more. An oak marble gall in my garden
   swims like a planet to me on the lawn
I don't cut very often, where moths rise from my sleep.
   Golf clubs are left by a low wall to be read
like the books we put out on a camping table
   in summer that wanderers came to read
without a word, and one without looking asked if we owned
   any old cameras, old, the better to see the world.

Here, where litter is not proverbial, a dropped Evian
    bottle marks the end either of single-use plastic
or us, two different maps of a thing
    on this map, given the slightest spin.
A neighbour I have never yet met looks a little lost
    as if he had turned three times and fifty years
had passed and the concrete crumbling at the edge
    of an otherwise well-kept drive was a cause of fear.
He might have taken a lead for a walk
    instead of a dog. *Morning*, I say, despite
my allergy, and he accepts it is morning with a nod.
    In Britain, that is sufficient to observe *l'esprit
des loix*, the invisible compact with anarchy
    that means the lost can draw, if not comfort, then
the pleasures of wearing fancy dress wherever
    they are, no matter what clothes they have on:
our best hope is a common-law bohemia.
    I toss a rusty nail I find on the footpath
into the green bin and the promise of recycling:
    utter change makes the street quiet. *Wohin der Weg?*
a stranger asks. *Kein Weg! Ins Unbetretene.*

Lord of Misrule

for Ian Marchant

Throwing up at the result of that referendum
My hot graffiti dripping from Parliament
    I bequeath thee shitte
Spamming every feed and trending now
The remedy, I say to the tired Christ
Slack in my skin
Is to be drunk, 'on wine, poetry or virtue, as you wish'
Preferably all three at once.
O for some Weimar easy virtue, given wisely
To snuff the insolence of office out
And dance a tango
Through their sober death.
I mean to teach these suits morality.

After a dunk in the Thames, black as oil,
I board my Zeppelin.
Far below, the city streets are floes of fire.
Pepys runs to bury his wheel of Parmesan cheese.
He, at least, takes my advice.

You are invited to the Feast of Fools.
Come dressed as the century,
Each of you a prophecy.
I will supply a little theatre.

Pale mummers, their tongues all told,
Haunt year zero:
Remind you that the dead can live
And will perform for food.
Will Kemp in his cap and bells
Dances a morris to Primal Scream
And conjures a crocus from broken earth.

The homeless, housed in Kensington
Drop pennies into the cups of royal rough sleepers
Cold on their thrones.
Those who once made money out of money
Even in 'crisis'
Find life in laying a hedge of hazel and willow
In the Midlands style.
I thought er wuz jed, one says, audible
Tears in the voice he has found in his blood.
I thought er wuz jed, an the spudgucks n'all
But they ay, they ay
Er's in this wand, an the spudgucks n'all.

Our revels last three days of night.
The players breed with the crowd.
When at last the lights go out
I let a full breast slip from my dress,
Dance with the living and the dead
Our mouths at our necks
Until Albion shudders its *petite mort*.

The suits drop their jaws, enlightened.

Shh. Go easy on that hungover head.
There are those who would hang us by an ankle
Until we bleed dry.
I play myself as a Tarot card
To see their fear eye to eye.

They will trespass at dawn
To drag me from my enseamèd bed
In the name of the crime they've dressed as the law
And ungratefully frame my jest as offence.
Someone will shout: My poor fool is hanged
But I will wink
From the gallows
When they think
I am dead.

Europa

We are estranged:
a people spoken of
as if in story.
Our existence moot
even to ourselves.

Who are these figures
behind our faces
and whose faces
are these our own?

Our stars are scattered
kingcups, light spilt
like certain fate
for we the lost to find
and build our firmament.

Our beautiful are still beautiful
but cold as fresh
statues waiting
for the warmth of blood.

We hold world office,
our intent as yet unknown.

We are old: we feel
that in our bones
and the noises
of our siren islands.
There are voices
on the air: are they
our own? Our mouths
are silent nestling crows
gaping to be fed.

Our sounds require
their dark interpreters.
Our spectres tell our young
we come from over the sea.
This element, this movement
between, this flood
of our speech
seeking us out.

We wake to reports
of a boat capsized
beyond the horizon.
We assemble in hope
as if in sight of ourselves.

A child washes ashore
with her gift of tongues.

She is alive.

A March Nest

A tilt of the light and I wake with a twig in my mouth,
building between the shoots and reeds I'd laid
in the quick of instinct, at work between the light.
Last night I met my mate, who laid her shape
to mine and gave my breath a tide as full
as any moon can hold, which rises as I build.

I met her as the space I braid to bear
the shape I dreamed, who shared my body's warmth
and weave: moss from ruins worked from stone:
the jade of lichen flourished from a fallen wand:
leaves that gave the dead their shade before
they fell, sown as gifts from the old year:
the yarn of grasses wound with fur and hair
bright with the animal they have shed: feathers
lighter than infant breath, bound with the thread
of a cobweb teased from a pool of thorns: daub
drawn from a spawning pond, wattled with the silk
of a sow-thistle, a seed-head blown by the wind:
the down of lamb's ear carded by bees: the soft
gold of morning cast in a lost ring.

The bulb of the sun swells in the earth I work
above, turning the air to smooth the cup
for the clutch that makes a chorus in my blood
like dawn. Calls pair across the waking
wood and ply between my own, for life
to come: the sung to, like the singer, unseen.

Second Best Bed

Her body has risen from my side:
I lie as if stunned by woman's
creation. As her shadow passed over
my eyes, still closed, I felt the eclipse
of our lives in the dawn of invention.

I am no more here than her soft absence
pressed like a flower between the leaves
of our linen, or this, my lettered tongue:
no more than a chrysalis in your hand
astir in the bed of its making.

Sky Burial

Not quite asleep, or dead
but laid out flush to mountain cloud

I ask for you, as if sick
with love stretched too thin

and you lean from the slant-bright sky
unreal as a remedy

and heal me, still, though you
are the sky that begins to chew

the numb leather of my skin
anaesthetic as a kiss

that lulls my flesh into air,
bones into breath

the raven rides to carrion.
The balm of your tongue

licks the orbit of my skull
as bears were said to shape their young

from the formless matter of their birth
and this body left for the birds returns

from the mouths of the wind
that found and fed on its scattering

and the rushing sky speaks in its nerve
as a gift your absence sends as love

that wakes my body's offering
to the tearing at its origin

that loosens and lifts me from the earth
to blow me back in the rite of words.

Don't Ask

Your iris is enough to obsess the dead:
and the dead, obsessed, already stare
through sunlight slowly dialling the air
around your flesh, every word I've bled

from the wound of what I never said
with the dead too close for me to dare,
with you so fixed in their listening glare:
they wait, lips at your skin, to be fed.

The dead obsess where the living stay too long,
as I have stayed, no less obsessed, my eyes
adoring yours, teaching the dead their bliss.

They breathe through the fracture of my wrong,
move with the tongue that tells no lies,
follow my love to your bed as we kiss.

Fogou

For breath, an air borrowed from the earth
dug to snuff the wick of the sun.

The silence that you hear is blood:
the bow of the dark to the string of your gut.

Your eyes are closed and see by stone:
clearer the colder and deeper you go.

The door is shut. You find your love,
the voice interred in the cleft of your own.

The only way out: your open mouth,
the creep too narrow to enter.

Mg: A Biography

Around twenty grams in each human skeleton –
about the same as the weight of the soul
according to Dr. Duncan MacDougall –
and no less essential: the spirit as magnesium.

We're slow to see what we can't live without:
Joseph Black first discerned the element
that, in 1792, Anton Rupprecht
called austrium after his native home,
and Humphry Davy first made pure in 1808 –
the metal he called magnium.

An element always slips its name.
This cousin of silver-white crystalline ore
lives the wisdom of flesh and bone
whether or not we know
the extract from its natural state.

We tap its latent brilliance for light,
but its silence translates the sun:
a single atom of this metal
powers each molecule of chlorophyll.

It is fundamental to life on earth.
Almost too precious to touch with a word.

Chess Metaphysic

It is too still to speak, and that is right:
        what comes next can only come
out of the ecstasy of my attention.
        I imply you as we play.

A lack of patience and the game will slip:
        as if I gave myself an hour
to solve and begin my life again.
        That's no way to let it live.

Your move implies that I am here,
        arranged in moves that I have made:
the visible order of invisible forms
        that shape the moves that we will make.

We watch for what we might not see,
        even within the ecstatic field
to which, for now, our minds belong.
        How easy it is to miss the truth.

To play you proves the tact of thought,
        but only one of us need be human.
Outside the game, a stranger sees
        carved enigmas on a chequered board.

Scenery

Between the shadow-green that drinks
his body and deepens him as wilding
grows he finds a human frame:
planes of oak with mitred joints
square the hollow of a stage,
its boards a floor across the brook
that gashes the combe and pours the sun:
he is speechless and alone
but for the burring insect mass
that weighs with the wings of the wood
at his ear: *who or what is natural here?*

He moves the way a human would,
enters the scene downstage right:
his clothes are a sudden burden to him
and he lets the chiffchaffs carry them off:
blood and breath, bare as bone
he mounts the stripped timber scaffold
over the running otherworld:
he drinks until his shadow flows
in green and dares to play the truth:
he lifts his skull as if to speak,
steps through the curtain of the air.

At English Bicknor

a knuckle three times   at the door, 1 a.m.
and I let it in   without rising from the bed
a well-dressed man   a tawny owl for a head

tilting at the neck   to level its eyes
with the clockwork walk   of the body it rides
halting towards me   on the beam of its gaze

a scritch in the flesh   and the dark is here
the call of silence   comes so clear
I am a nest full of mouths   open at the ear

Daemon

Who is this on a thread
like a spider through the air
when the spider is missing from its weft?

The sun arrives to find him
like the bee arrives at clover
and finds a shadow growing
in the heaven of its garden
honeysuckle round its throat
opening low lilac cries
between the trembling lungs of grass

Whose hand set the head
that dropped like fruit
in the crooked shoulder of the apple tree?

Come closer to its moving mouth
and soft as moisture rising
through its moss you might hear
the slow lapping of a spirit's tongue
make your bones soft as sound

Consistori del Gai Saber

for Philip Allott

Tell those who come they have to find
the sound of knowing for themselves,
as I did, three hundred
and seventy-seven moons ago.
It is nothing so fixed as the earth
at the centre of the spheres (which, mark me,
is a truth that will loosen like a slip
of the tongue) but the maker of fact, the spell
that makes you a fiction, howbeit real.
But I'm going too fast. It begins
with overhearing the dead
in the living. What else is a word
but a ghost sent feeling its way,
the centuries passed on your breath?
And in this, the feat of surprise.
When a stranger speaks and it sounds
upon you a promise of being
that it keeps as it touches the stem
of your fate, something like a voice
that you love. That is the invisible body
of our wandering college, to which anyone
can belong – if they choose. For me,
born without money or precedent
but yes, loved, and my weird strong enough,
one dead *dictador* became my teacher.
The music in words can be its own song.
I imagine him lit by brandy and candle,
the room drunk, for a moment, on language,
and he half-aware that those who listen

have not yet been born. Look for the signs
that tell you the student has heard the dead
and plays for them as they would for a friend.
Look for signs that the dead have heard.
This is not solemn: the *violeta d'aur*
has to be earned, as does the ear
of those who come after. They, like the language,
deserve our best benefaction.

                              Listen –
the golden oriole is back, and arcs
the air with his whistle. He is a *joglar*
like me, the magus of this morning's taroc.
Look how the hard-at-work and the self-absorbed
alike ignore the pageant of his arrival.
But let's not be doleful: there's a joke
in the tragic mask of their loss as old
as laughter itself, just as a prude
is the dupe of sex, and the sober
are fools of reason. Unwilling clowns
are clowns nonetheless – better to choose
to play. Our students should have a stomach
for paradox, and impatience only with the absence
of love. We have the freedom of fallen
beings. Think not of fresco devils
nor huddled angels with blue-washed wings
but their nameless painter at work in the temple
of their imagining – the art in the thought
of transfiguring – who wears the horned brow
of an ecstasy older than Christendom.
Forgive my heresy, but we who perform
have a habit of asking to be
forgiven in the very trespass of our voice.
We belong to no class but our calling.
Our ways are promiscuous as language,

over which we raise the sign of Eros.
When I speak it's to kiss my absent
lover, who may not even be human.
I like a music that reaches where speech
is forbidden unless it speaks in wonder.
That is the beginning and the end
of our learning. If you can hear my smile
it's because I savour the romance of knowledge,
even the wound of its sounding.
Listen: those spheres are moving.
I have told you some secrets, maybe
said too much. But I never forget
my audience – nor those who might be
overhearing. Come. Step through this curtain
and into the sun. The world is young.
I find what I learn from the oriole pleasing.

Quest

Too idle to quest
except with a book
whose leaves draw figures
from the sheet of the air

I send them instead
through a blink of the sun
with a fold of my breath
in a paper moth

to find the flame
that weeps from the dark
slight as a candle
in a world snuffed out

and when they return
and you ask for proof
there is frost on my skin
and the book has burned

Notes

Gramarye: Gramarye is occult learning, magic; related to the words grammar, glamour and grimoire.

A Poppet: A poppet is a doll, or effigy used in witchcraft.

Labels for the Exhibition of an Hitherto Private Cabinet of Masks: Wyre – the Wyre Forest, Worcestershire and Shropshire. Devilfish – an old seafarers' folk name for the octopus (also applied to other sea-creatures). Candia – the name of Crete and its capital under the Venetocracy (thirteenth to the seventeenth century CE).

Metaphysician: Chiron – the teacher and healer centaur of Pelion, whose name means 'hand'. Da'at (also da'ath or daath) – 'knowledge', as a mediatory, animating, continually renewing potency.

Tree Script: Amongst other tree- and alphabet-lore, this poem draws on – but does not reproduce – aspects of the medieval Beth-Luis-Nion tree-alphabet that names the letters of the ancient ogham script. 'The Moon owns it': the entry for the willow in Nicholas Culpeper's *Complete Herbal* (1653).

Archaeopteryx: A fossilised feathered reptile, named in 1861 from the Greek meaning 'ancient wing'. Long viewed as the 'first bird' (or Urvogel in Germany, where its remains were found), it lived in the late Jurassic period, around 147 million years ago.

Tuisto: The poem plays on the speculative etymology of Tuisto, which relates the name of the mysterious god recorded in Tacitus to Proto-Germanic words implying 'double' or 'doubling', as well as to Tiwaz, the putative antecedent of the Anglo-Saxon deity Tiw (whose name survives in 'Tuesday'). *eorþe*: (Old English) earth.

Modranect: According to Bede's *De temporum ratione* (c. 725 CE), the pre-Christian, Old English name for the night at the turn of the year on 25 December: literally, 'the night of the Mothers'.

Transhumanist Glitch: 'Transhuman' first appears in English in H.F. Cary's translation of Dante's *Divine Comedy* (1814) – the version that the Romantics read: 'Words may not tell of that transhuman change'. The lines in Dante – where the poet compares the beatific vision to Glaucus's transfiguration, on eating a magic herb, into an oracular god – are 'Trasumanar significar per verba / non si poria' (*Paradiso* I. 70-1). In 1951 Julian Huxley used the word 'transhumanism' to mean 'the idea of humanity attempting to overcome its limitations and to arrive at a fuller fruition'. Now the word is associated with the work of Ray Kurzweil and (in the definition given by Singularity 2050) 'a movement devoted to using technologies to transcend biology and enhance human capabilities'. 'H+' has been used as a symbol of transhumanism in the latter sense.

The Ape at the End of the World: *Summa sapientiae*: (Latin) 'the sum of all wisdom'.

Interval: The word as used in the poem includes its musicological sense: the difference in pitch between two tones.

Sakadas at Delphi: Sakadas of Argos was the first winner of the musical contests (*mousikoi agones*) staged at the Pythian Games at Delphi, c. 586 BCE – and went on to win the contest several times. The epigraph is the title of a work published in 1597 by the English composer Thomas Morley (1557-1602).

Beorma: 'Beorma' is the name commonly given to the legendary Anglo-Saxon founder of Birmingham, which – as 'Beorma-inga-ham' – may mean 'home of the people of Beorma'. The poem also plays on etymological patterns that suggest connections between the origins of the name Birmingham and those of numerous settlements around the English midlands. Rising at its southern periphery, the River Cole runs through and beyond the city.

Unconscious Minister: The title (like the epigraph) is taken from Thomas De Quincey's *Confessions of an English Opium-Eater* (1821), in which he refers to the Oxford Street druggist that first sold him opium as the 'unconscious minister of celestial pleasures'.

Dérive: 'Dérive' comes from the French for 'drifting', and relates to the psychogeographical practice, as promoted by Guy Debord, of traversing urban or semi-urban terrain in a deliberately experimental attitude open to the defamiliarising effects of any aspect of that environment. *'l'esprit des loix'* – 'the spirit of the laws', alludes to the work of political theory and comparative law *De l'esprit des loix* by Montesquieu (1748), which includes a study of the English constitution. The German at the end of the poem is from Goethe's *Faust* (1808): 'What is the way?' asks Faust; 'There is no way! Into the untrodden...', Mephistopheles replies. (p. 79)

Lord of Misrule: The Lord of Misrule – here reimagined – was an official of late medieval England appointed to oversee the Christmas revelries, including masques and feasts. *'I bequeath thee shitte'* is a line spoken by Sathanas (the Devil-Fool) to Christ in the medieval mystery play *The Temptation of Christ*. To be drunk 'on wine, poetry or virtue, as you wish', derives from 'Enivrez-vous' by Baudelaire. Will Kemp, the clown, performed for a time with Shakespeare's company the Lord Chamberlain's Men. He once morris-danced from London to Norwich in nine days. Black Country dialect: jed – dead / spudgucks – sparrows.

Europa: Composed 24 June 2016. The goddess Europa was brought to Crete from Phoenicia by Zeus. 'dark interpreters': alludes to an oneiric figure in Thomas De Quincey's *Suspiria De Profundis*.

Second Best Bed: The title is taken from the enigmatic term in Shakespeare's will: 'Unto my wyf I gyve my second best bed with the furniture'.

Fogou: A fogou is a form of prehistoric underground passage-chamber found in Cornwall.

Mg: A Biography: In 2018 the Institute for Sustainable Futures at Birmingham City University organised a symposium on the applications of magnesium in technology and industry. I was invited to compose a poem to mark the occasion, which formed the basis of the poem here.

Consistori del Gai Saber: The poem draws on the history of the Consistori del Gai Saber – 'Consistory of Joyous Knowledge' – a poetic academy for the cultivation of lyric poetry, founded in Toulouse in 1323. Occitan: *dictador* – poet / *violeta d'aur* – the 'golden violet', the prize for the best poet at the consistory's annual poetry contest / *joglar* – performer, minstrel, etymologically connected with the Juggler, or Magus, of tarot. 'Weird' is used here as a noun, principally in its older meaning, from the Old English *wyrd:* fate, or becoming.

Acknowledgements

My thanks to the editors of the journals and anthologies in which several of these poems, or versions of them, first appeared: *The Hudson Review, The Poetry Review, Wild Court, Poetry Birmingham Literary Journal, Consilience, Lyrical Aye, New Boots and Pantisocracies, Writing Lives Together* (University of Leicester, 2017) and *This Is Not Your Final Form: Poems about Birmingham* (The Emma Press, 2017).

'Sakadas at Delphi' was commissioned by Birmingham City University for the opening of the new Royal Birmingham Conservatoire in March 2018, and 'Beorma' was commissioned for the inauguration of Sir Lenny Henry as Chancellor of the University in November 2016. 'Terroir' was commissioned for the Overhear Poetry app in September 2019, and responds to the location of Connolly's Wine Merchants, Livery Street, Birmingham. 'Unconscious Minister' was commissioned by the Centre for New Writing at the University of Leicester as part of the 'Writing Lives Together: Romantic and Victorian auto/ biography' project. 'Second Best Bed' was composed while I was Poet in Residence at Anne Hathaway's Cottage as part of the Stratford-upon-Avon Poetry Festival in 2016. 'Gramarye' was shortlisted for the Montreal International Poetry Prize 2020.

Warm thanks to Jane Commane for her energy, enthusiasm and generosity, including the opportunity to attend the Nine Arches Press retreat at Hartsop to work on this book; to Eloise (for telling me her dream), Freya and Karen; to Matthew Scudamore, who (with curious synchronicity) told me about *Impro: Improvisation and the Theatre* by Keith Johnstone, with its chapter on 'Masks and Trance'; to the Zellig poetry group, with whom some of the poems here were first aired; and for insight, empathy and good humour in conversation and correspondence about poetry, Jonathan Davidson, Patrick McGuinness, Dana Gioia and Jim Crace.